GC

A Min

GOLF

A Mind Game

Richard Butler and **Peter Galvin**
with illustrations by **Geo Parkin**

QUEENSGATE PUBLICATIONS

First published in 1999
by Queensgate Publications
Cookham, Berkshire

ISBN 1-902655-03-6

A catalogue record of this book is available from the British Library.

Cover design by Charlie Webster
Book design by Production Line, Minster Lovell, Oxford
Production by Landmark Consultants, Princes Risborough, Buckinghamshire
Printed in Finland by WSOY

The idea for this book was formed in a bar in Palmerston North, New Zealand. I would like to thank my friend, Bill Chote, for helping me to have the idea. It's a pity he doesn't remember it, but thanks anyway Bill.

Peter Galvin
Leeds, England

'The only important judge of yourself is you' *(page 70)*

Contents

Introduction   8

Know your clubs   12
Your golfing profile   14
Setting goals   16
Effective practice   18
Game planning   20
Making decisions   22
Learning through feedback   24
Increasing awareness   26
Trigger words   28
Key images   30
The pre-shot routine   32
Focus   34
Keeping in the present   36
Switching on and off   38
Focusing on the target   40
Positive thinking   42
Healthy thoughts   44
Stay calm   46
Relaxed breathing   48

Your mind's eye   50

A positive frame of mind   52

Play to your strengths   54

The lighter side   56

Act as if   58

Personalise your shots   60

Making the difficult easy   62

Savour the experience   64

Symbolism   66

Playing with paradox   68

Partners   70

Getting to know yourself   72

Your golfing self   74

Your learning style   76

Know your feelings   78

Disperse the red mist   80

Problem? What problem?   82

A philosopher on the course   84

Take response-ability   86

Dealing with pressure   88

Dealing with defeat   90

Pursuing your limits   92

The perfect golfer?   94

Index   96

Introduction

'This game is great and very strange.'   Seve Ballesteros

Golf is inherently a technical sport. As golfers, we try to improve our technical skills by poring over a huge range of magazines and books available, or by watching the masters on video. Alternatively, we might spend hours on the driving range or perhaps look to a professional coach for guidance.

Yet we still grub shots; we still hook viciously to the left; we still miss the two-foot putt. As Arnold Palmer astutely reflected: 'Golf is deceptively simple yet endlessly complicated.'

Undoubtedly, there are techniques the golfer can acquire that will significantly increase the chances of hitting the ball in the right direction. However, as with so many other things in life, there are no certainties. If there were then the best technical golfer would win every time.

So if we are to master our inconsistencies, then we must be prepared to experiment with new thinking, to apply creativity and to hone our psychological approach to the game.

In recent years, mastery of the mental game has emerged as a significant factor in determining how well we play. And you don't need to take our word for it; witness these thoughts from some of the world's greatest golfers:

'Ninety percent of golf is played from the shoulders up.'   Arnold Palmer

'Once you've got the physical bit then it's all in the mind.'   Nick Faldo

'Golf is a game played on a five inch course – the distance between your ears.'
                    Bobby Jones

If the correct mental approach is so essential to the top players, it raises the question of how much more we can improve our game by exploring our psychological potential.

The aim of this book is to invite you to try out new ideas, to seek to improve your performance and to open up new possibilities. To encourage you to be, in essence, your own psychological coach.

Golf, the most solitary of sports, lends itself ideally to the notion of the performer as his or her own coach. There are no team mates, no-one on the sidelines offering us encouragement; there is no manager deciding when and how often to practice, what equipment to use, when to have lessons. Golf is an individual sport. We decide what to sacrifice in order to improve our performance. Ultimately, when we play – or compete – we are playing against ourselves.

But there is no easy route to improving our mental approach to the game. Arnold Palmer's comment that 'golf is almost a science, yet it is a puzzle with no answer' might equally be applied to psychological principles. In this book, we have tried to unravel the complexities by presenting ideas in an accessible way. By singling out the key thoughts and illustrating them with diagrams, cartoons and quotes, we have sought to demystify the principles. Ultimately, we have tried to bring to life what it is that you can do to improve your performance, present to you the necessary psychological skills and then invite you to sample them to see if they make a difference to your game.

The book is a collection of short chapters, each focusing on one particular aspect of the game which might be improved given the correct mental approach. We hope that it might serve as something of a quick-reference manual, perhaps 'dipped into' whether you are at home, on the practice ground or out enjoying a round. It does not have to be read from cover to cover to derive benefit from the text.

It is split broadly into three sections:

Performance

Psychological techniques to improve golfing skills and technique. This is about seeking to be good at our game. It is about being in the C zone, and applying the following principles: Confidence, Concentration, Calmness, Control.

Enjoyment

Adopting psychological skills that raise the sense of fun or pleasure from golf. This is seeking to be happy with our game and forms the second part of the book, where the creative side is encouraged. As Albert Einstein said: 'Imagination is more important than knowledge.'

Self-awareness

Self-discovery through applying psychological thought to the way the game is played. This is seeking to be happy with ourselves. Golf is a microcosm of life. How we play golf reflects something of our personality. As John Updike described: 'Golf seems like a magic mirror; an outward projection of an inner self.' If we take the time to study the way we react during a round of golf, we can begin to discover things about ourselves that we were previously unaware of. Golf encourages reflection. It is a means of understanding ourselves.

Grantland Rice persuasively suggested that 'golf gives you an insight into human nature – yours as well as that of your opponent.' Alan Shapiro went somewhat further. He described how, once a golfer has experienced the highs – the successes – he realises that he has 'stumbled upon some dark, deep secret that it is not just about hitting a golf ball straight and long. He knows that he has accessed part of himself that lies outside the commonplace, daily world of ego-driven material pursuits and athletic conquests.'

In addition to acting as a medium for self-awareness, golf – or improving our golf – can also facilitate self-development. The psychological techniques we develop are also appropriate to other aspects of life. Decision making, visualisation, relaxation, confidence building and so forth are all skills that can be applied to a job interview, a key-note speech or an important business meeting. The important thing to remember is that the real test of golf, and life, is not keeping out of the rough but finding the best way out once we are there.

So this is not a book designed to give advice on specific problems, it is a book which will foster the art of asking ourselves good questions and giving ourselves good advice. That advice will improve both our game and our feel for the game, as well as the way we feel about ourselves.

Know your clubs

'Golf is a game whose aim is to hit a very small ball into an even smaller hole, with weapons ill-designed for the purpose.'   Winston Churchill

Key thought

It is a poor workman who blames his tools. To do so locates the problem, or source of trouble, beyond him. This is sometimes referred to as externalising. It reduces what we can do to change things. Perhaps it is the good workman who gets the best out of the tools he has, no matter how modest or second hand they are. Both our attitude to our clubs and the quality of the clubs themselves make a difference to our game. Knowing our clubs can have all round benefits. It may enhance our performance, increase our sense of enjoyment and further our understanding of ourselves.

• Performance

Understand the clubs' potential. What is each club capable of in our hands?

Tommy Horton suggests hitting 20 shots with a club. Ignore the five worst

and five best shots and average the distance of the remaining ten. This gives a rough personal estimate of distance for that club. In this way we can discover what distance each club can be relied on to give us.

David Leadbetter suggests that if you know the distance you tend to reach with each club then you don't ever have to hit too hard in trying to get distance, you simply take an extra club.

Perceive the clubs' properties. Notice how they feel and sound when you swing them, whether they make the ball ping or thud.

- Enjoyment
  Know your clubs' temperament. Do some clubs perform better under different circumstances? Which clubs relish the cold days, which ones the wet days or the hot spells? This is a way of establishing more control over our game. It is empowering.

'In lightning, hold up a one iron and walk. Even God can't hit a one iron.'   Lee Trevino

Assess your clubs' character. Choose the most sympathetic club for the shot. Which clubs do we put our trust in? Which can we count on to do the job we want?

Personalise your favourite clubs with pet names, such as 'cannon', 'my beauty', 'Excalibur', 'Marilyn' and so on.

- Self-awareness
  How does a club make you feel? Nervous, intimidated, bold, confident, relaxed? What is it about the club that generates this feeling? It might reflect some aspect of your personality. Thus feeling bold with the driver in your hand might reflect your fearlessness. Feeling intimidated by the three iron might reflect your need not to fail.

It is of course beneficial to try and create a positive relationship with each club. Is it possible to develop positive thoughts for those clubs we loathe? Try considering what advantages each club has for us. Put your need in the club. Share the responsibility for the shot you want with the club you have chosen. Try completing the statement: 'I need you to...' For example: 'I need you to get me out of the bunker.'

13

Your golfing profile

'Good scoring in golf involves, in addition to swinging the clubs correctly, analysis, judgement, planning and decisions.'
Edward Chui

Key thought

To play golf well we have to rely on a range of skills or attributes. A good performance consistently starts with an understanding of those attributes that are important to our own game. We then assess our abilities for each of the skills and visualise how we would like to be. A 'Performance Profile' enables us to develop a map of our abilities highlighting our strengths and weaknesses. It also gives us a notion of which qualities we feel we need in order to perform well.

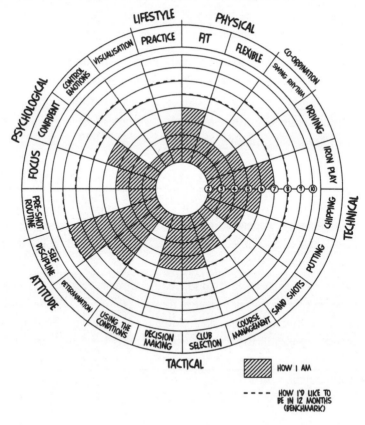

14

A typical Performance Profile contains:

1. A raft of attributes or qualities considered important: these are written on the rim of the Profile.
2. A personal assessment on each of these attributes: these are the shaded areas.
3. A measure of what would make you the golfer you'd like to be in 12 months time: the dashed line

To establish your own Performance Profile think about your ideal golfer and consider what it is they do that enables them to perform at their best. These are what you perceive to be qualities or attributes of a top performance. Make a note of these qualities. They are what you personally believe to be important and are not necessarily the views of coaches, partners or friends.

You might find it useful to try to consider qualities from each of the following categories:

PHYSICAL: eg. strong, flexible, fit, powerful

CO-ORDINATION: eg. balance, rhythm, flow, posture

TECHNICAL: eg. weight distribution, bunker escape, fading, drawing the ball, downhill putting, short game, iron play, driving, swing.

TACTICAL: eg. planning, club selection, course management

ATTITUDINAL: eg. competitive, disciplined, determination

PSYCHOLOGICAL: eg. confident, cool, focused, preparation

LIFESTYLE: eg. practice, personal health

From your list select the 20 most important qualities for you and write these on your Profile rim. Then, rate yourself out of ten where you judge yourself to be on each quality at the present moment, on a scale where '0' indicates no aptitude or ability at all and '10' indicates a very high degree of competence. Shade in your score on the Profile.

Finally, using the same 0-10 scale, try and rate where you would like to be in 12 months time. Mark this score on the Profile as a dashed line or in a different colour. This is your benchmark rating, providing a measure of the progress you intend to make over the coming months. It is a good idea to rate yourself on a regular basis so that the Profile acts as a monitor of the progress you are making.

'Golf and sex are about the only things you can enjoy without being good at either.'
Jimmy Demaret

Setting goals

'In golf you're always breaking a barrier. When you bust it, you set yourself a little higher barrier and try to break that one.'

Jack Nicklaus

Key thought

The best goals should always:

1. Be about PERFORMANCE [what we can do to improve the chances of a good outcome], rather than the outcome itself. For example, goals such as 'relax my shoulders' or 'pitch at the flag' are far better than ones such as 'win the tournament' or 'birdie all the par 5s' because they focus on what we can do to improve the chances of the outcome we want. Focusing on the outcome alone provides a useful challenge, but it is not a useful goal because it does not focus on what we need to do.

2. Be REALISTIC not over-ambitious. We need a target that is achievable rather than one that is clearly beyond our capability. 'Sink all the 20 foot putts' is not a realistic goal. To play to our own par, on the other hand, is realistic. If our average round is 36 over par then we might rub out par on the scorecard and pencil in our own. Then a Par Three becomes a Par Five; a Par Four becomes a Par Six and so on.

3. Be under CONTROL. We must be in charge of our game, and not be dependent upon outside circumstances in order to succeed. Thus a goal such as 'to beat my partner' is not an effective one because we cannot control

16

what sort of round he or she might have. Our partner's score is not under our control; what is under our control is our own game.

4. Be POSITIVE. Avoid words such as 'not' or 'don't' when phrasing the goal. Such negatives have a habit of reminding us what we shouldn't do. Thus if the phrase 'don't tense up on my swing' is our goal, then we are more likely to tense up. It is much better to state our target positively, for example: 'keep my shoulders relaxed during the swing.'

PSYCHOLOGICAL PRINCIPLE:
Think BIG but start SMALL

When studying the Performance Profile, identify qualities that might be considered to be areas of weakness in your game. These might be qualities where you have given yourself a low rating or where there is a discrepancy between your rating as you perceive yourself now and where you would like to be in 12 months time.

Consider what you can do in order to improve your performance in this area. This might mean some research into technical manuals, observing others or seeking advice from a coach. Describe the action required of yourself and summarise it as a goal. This is sometimes best achieved by completing the statement: 'I aim to...'

Thus a goal might be: 'I aim to keep my back swing slow and smooth on each shot.'

Remember to keep your statement within the watchwords described: PERFORMANCE, REALISTIC, CONTROL and POSITIVE. In the example above, the goal covers all these parameters:

1. PERFORMANCE: slow and smooth backswing.
2. REALISTIC: achievable on each shot.
3. CONTROL: it is something I can do, and is not dependent on other people.
4. POSITIVE: it contains no negative phrases.

17

Effective practice

'The more I practice, the luckier I become.'   Gary Player

Key thought

The difference between practice on the range and playing out on the course is vast. In practice the aim often seems to be to hit as many balls as possible, whereas the challenge of the game is to hit as few balls as possible.

When we practice we tend to use the same club repeatedly, playing the same shot endlessly, whereas on the course we change clubs each shot and vary the stroke to the conditions. In practice we tend to dispense with any pre-shot routine but then try to maintain one on the course. We face the same hazards repeatedly on the driving range but face an almost infinite variety of possibilities on the course. Thus practice and playing might be thought of as very different activities. No wonder it sometimes feels that we cannot transfer our hard work on the range to playing the game itself.

If something isn't working we have a tendency to practice harder doing the same thing. We may therefore groove errors into our game. But the more practice simulates the way we play on the course the less we face the problem of transferring good practice shots to our game.

PSYCHOLOGICAL PRINCIPLE:
Quality not quantity

- Don't play the same shot over and over again. There's never a second chance during the game.
- A score is generally made up of a third of full shots and two thirds less than full shots. Jack Nicklaus knew this. For years he was never the world's best at long drives yet he was constantly top of the list for fewest putts. Perhaps 70% of shots during a round are from within 100 yards of the flag. It makes sense to practice these.
- Practice as if you are on the course. For each practice shot, try to go through the same pre-shot routine as we would on the course.

'All my life I've tried to hit practice shots with great care. I try to have a clear-cut purpose in mind on every swing. I always practice as I intend to play.'   Jack Nicklaus

- Driving: decide on a variety of distances to hit, rather than the furthest possible. Practice fading and drawing; simulate course conditions with imaginary trees, hedges and water hazards.
- Short game: practice chipping, pitching and bunker shots in equal amounts. Keep scores of how many you land within 3 foot of the hole in a session and try to improve in future sessions.
- Long putts: on the course, long putts often fall short. It's not accuracy but pace that is important. Practice hitting balls to the edge of the green or just onto the fringe from different parts of the green.
- Short putts: success with short putts is about accuracy and line. Firmly hit, a putt will usually go in. Scatter five balls randomly within two feet of the hole and aim to hit each into the hole. Only once you have achieved 100% success do you increase the distance from the hole to four feet and further.
- Warm-up putting before play: scatter balls randomly around the hole. Start putting nearest and work to furthest away. Visualise the stroke, the path of the ball to the hole and the sound of the ball hitting the cup. Limit the number of practice shots until your rhythm, tempo and touch feel right. Then stop, irrespective of how many you have sunk.

Game planning

'Seve Ballesteros goes after a golf course the way a lion goes after a zebra' Jim Murray

Key thought

Being proactive enhances the pleasure we get from an activity and establishes control over our direction. We take charge of our own destiny. Not taking control means we are at the mercy of whim, or of other people's wishes. In golf, if we adopt a game plan it establishes in broad terms how we intend the round to go.

PSYCHOLOGICAL PRINCIPLE
Control the game rather than let the game control you

- A game plan will generally have a guiding principle. This forms the bedrock of all decision-making as we complete the course. The guiding principle might well differ between rounds.

- A broad game plan might have a key word as its guiding principle. For example: cautious; adventurous; risky; controlled; powerful; polished; professional; enjoyment; shrewd; aggressive; wing it.
- Consider what actions are associated with the guiding principle you choose:

  Risky might mean taking a chance or doing the unexpected.

  Professional might mean playing a measured game.

  Enjoyment might imply trying out new approaches to a hole.
- The game plan should underpin your approach to each shot, so try to keep in mind in advance of that shot what it is you are aiming to achieve. Thus drives, chips and putts can all be played riskily, or professionally, or for enjoyment – depending on your overall game plan.
- Try to stick to your game plan throughout the round whatever circumstances contrive against you.
- At the end of the round assess how successful you were in sticking to your game plan. Did you draw on it for each shot?
- Then assess what the game plan achieved for your golf. Did it improve your performance or increase the enjoyment? Did it help you discover something about yourself?

Making decisions

'Make realism the fifteenth club in your bag.'   Tommy Horton

Key thought

We may make many hundreds of decisions on the golf course. Many are made without our even being aware. We perhaps make choices that feel right instinctively and only after the event do we question our decision. There are other times we clearly make a choice to go for a spectacular shot rather than a winning one. We choose to go for glory. Sometimes they come off but more usually they end in dismal failure. Attacking golf is fine but attempting a risky shot tends to ruin the score.

'If you honestly assess your game and determine that you will hit the iron successfully nine out of ten times, and hit the driver to the green one time in ten, then the risk-reward calculation is obvious.'   Bob Rotella, Sports Psychologist

There is plenty of time and opportunity on the golf course for deliberation. This fact alone should improve our chances of making the right decision.

PSYCHOLOGICAL PRINCIPLE
Good decision-making relies on paying attention to the relevant details and selecting the option most likely to work.

Decision-making can be improved by reflecting on some of the following tips:
- Slow down before making a decision. Unlike many sports golf normally provides the time to ponder and be circumspect.

'Take the club out of your bag slowly.'   Corey Pavin

- These are some of the factors to weigh up in the decision-making process:
    1. The club for the distance
    2. Our success ratio with the club
    3. The context of the game
    4. Take a risk or a percentage shot
    5. The way the course is playing
    6. The weather

- Be clear about your objective: 'What am I aiming to do here?' It is a platitude, but the aim of golf is to get the ball into the hole with the fewest shots. Some players forget this and focus instead on trying out a new club, ironing out their swing or playing shots for effect.
- Examine the risk of the choice. Trying to reach the green on a Par Five with two risky long shots might be impossible for all but the best players. Why not go for two easier shots with the 3 wood and a pitch onto the green? This reduces the risk and probably increases the likelihood of being on the green in three.
- Make yourself the caddie. What would he or she suggest?
- Ask yourself: 'Where do I want to be when I play the next shot?' If you're good with the wedge, then is it possible to get within a wedge shot of the hole? Tom Kite is an expert with the sand wedge from 70 yards. Therefore he will often try to position himself 70 yards from the flag after two shots on a Par Five, giving himself an opportunity to play his strongest shot.
- What are the alternatives to your choice? Weigh up all the options and check out the plusses and minuses of each possible course of action.

In the end all choices carry risk and the decision we take might turn out to be the wrong one. But we don't have the benefit of hindsight; it's only the critics who can enjoy commenting on what we should have done. Maybe next time, before playing the shot, you should be your own critic.

Learning through feedback

'I know I'm getting better at golf because I'm hitting fewer spectators.'   Gerald R Ford

Key thought

If you are going to learn how to be a better golfer then you need to find ways of getting feedback on your performance. As a golfer, you are engaged in a learning cycle which goes something like this: you perform the shot; you have an idea of how you performed during that shot and on the basis of this you either make an alteration or you decide to repeat the same action. Getting quality feedback from someone is motivating: it gives you a clear sense of your current performance and motivates you to improve.

PSYCHOLOGICAL PRINCIPLE
Good quality feedback is essential in order to improve your performance. Lack of feedback is likely to sap your motivation.

- The most obvious method of getting feedback is through a close examination of your scorecard. By making positive and negative notes of your performance on the card you can set yourself targets for the next round or even the next hole. For example: 'My chipping was inconsistent. Target: try to improve consistency by putting more weight on my left foot.' Keep your scorecards and notice any changes, particularly those that are positive ones. This process is motivating.
- Another good source of feedback is your partner. But beware. If you want quality feedback then you must be clear about what you want your partner to comment upon. Ask them to be specific in their analysis and get them, if possible, to transform the fault into a positive target. For example: you ask your partner to look at why you are topping the ball. He says that he thinks you might be coming up too soon and that you ought to try looking at a piece of grass in front of the ball until he says 'look up'.
- The same applies when you give feedback to yourself: you must be specific about what is happening. Be frequent and be brief. Keep the conversation short and positive.

- Try increasing your body awareness by swinging with your eyes closed and sensing where the tension is in your body. This can help you interpret what and therefore how you are doing.
- Do you have access to a camcorder? A video of your swing can be an invaluable source of information.
- Even the sound of the club striking the ball can provide feedback. Ask yourself: 'how did that sound?' Aim for the same sound again. This exercise also clears the mind of unnecessary thoughts as you swing.
- Devise your own personal methods of feedback such as a rating system, record the number of fairway shots, record the number of putts. Anything that gives you the language to describe and therefore increase your sense of how you are performing constitutes good feedback.

Increasing awareness

'The one secret for any golfer trying to improve is to decide first which is his or her own correct way.'
                                                                                    John Jacobs

Key thought

Many great and successful golfers such as Arnold Palmer, Gary Player, Jim Furyk and Lee Trevino have taken great pride in knowing that their swings were not orthodox. We each have a swing that is unique to ourselves. Indeed, there really is no perfect swing; only a swing that is perfect for us. So forget about trying to make the perfect swing, but value and learn from your own. This means learning to listen to what our body is telling us.

PSYCHOLOGICAL PRINCIPLE
Different strokes for different folks

Tim Gallwey has emphasised the importance of developing an awareness of our actions. This strengthens our focus and encourages us to adjust our swing to increase its effectiveness.

Immediately following a shot...

• Notice the presence of any tension:
  – in your hands, forearms, neck, shoulders, feet
  – rate the degree of tension out of 10, with 10 being the most tense
  – try tensing the area by 1 point
  – try the swing at this level of tension
  – try out the shot at different ratings from 0 [relaxed] to 10 [tense]
  – select the level/rating which feels best

• Notice the weight of the club:
  – rate from 0 [heavy] to 10 [light]

• Notice your grip:
  – rate from 0 [tight] to 10 [light]. Some golfers suggest it should be no tighter than holding a tube of toothpaste.
  – practice shots at different ratings

'The only thing you should force in a golf swing is the club back into the bag.'

Byron Nelson

At the end of a round...

• Find a quiet time at home, sit back, shut your eyes and conjure up the round in every detail:
  – every shot you played
  – the lie of the ball
  – the club selected
  – how you felt
  – the conditions
  – your swing
  – how the shot turned out

Reflecting on the round in this way will develop a sense of awareness about your performance. When you next play your level of awareness will be heightened.

Trigger words

'Grip it and rip it.'   John Daley

Key thought

One word is worth a thousand instructions. Trigger words – or metaphors – elicit a required action or series of actions. They are personally meaningful and both focus attention and produce the desired action.

Unlike many sports where we react to a moving ball, in golf we are faced with a stationary ball. We are motionless as we stand over it and we make the decision to move into the backswing and begin the shot. This point can generate physical tension and mental paralysis which may lead us to freeze. Trigger words can kick us into action.

POSSIBLE TRIGGER WORDS
Cool Smooth Oily Springy Rooted Relaxed Explode
Gutsy Sharp Controlled Flowing

The best trigger words are:
- – phrased positively
- – short and succinct
- – personal and idiosyncratic [they express something to us]
- – expressed with conviction [may be emotionally loaded]
- – practised until they become automatic

Finding your own personal key words:
- Pick one action you'd like to make more consistent [eg. your perfect swing; chipping onto the green; pitching from a down slope].
- Describe the desired action in detail either by writing it down, describing it to another person or imagine describing the quality as a poet, paying attention to how, in your own mind, it should be played perfectly.
- Listen for any emotive, poignant words – words that are vivid, clear and best depict what you want to achieve. These words should be associated with the perfect action.

- Practice associating the trigger word as you begin addressing the ball. In this way it will become associated with the action and will serve to generate it when you might be under pressure. Get the club moving in response to the trigger word.

Key images

'He just exploded, like a clenched fist travelling down the track.'

Neill Allen of Bob Hayes

Key thought

Many golfers acquire names that conjure up an image and portray their game in a particular way: the white shark; the tiger; the white bear.

Having an image of ourselves on the golf course, or an image of how a particular shot should be played, allows us to act as if we are that image. We can call upon its special qualities to help us play the shot.

'He's like a gorilla off the tee.'

Billy Casper of Seve Ballesteros

Acquiring an image:

- Think about a quality you rely on and which serves you well on the golf course [eg. balance; shrewdness; calmness; aggression; power].
- Can you conjure up an image or picture of this quality? Often images from the animal kingdom are useful.
- Try to complete a sentence including this quality. For example: 'as cunning as a fox; as graceful as a swan.'
- Try to acquire images which are striking, vivid, dramatic and – most importantly – personal to you.
- Use the image to spark actions or feelings in the same way as trigger words. Conjure up the image just prior to the shot.

'Perhaps if I dyed my hair peroxide blonde and called myself the 'Great White Tadpole' people would take more notice of me.' Ian Woosnam

The pre-shot routine

'The more we ingrain a routine of setting up by repeatedly rehearsing a procedure on the driving range and in casual play, the less we will be likely to step out of line when it really matters.'

Seve Ballesteros

Key thought

Keeping a steady rhythm and pace can be difficult. Unexpected things happen. We spend time searching for a lost ball and feel we are holding up the group behind; we become agitated by the slow group ahead; we scramble to rake the sand after a bunker shot and putt the next shot too hastily. Instead of being calm and composed we feel disrupted and play our shots without the necessary focus.

Having a set routine we follow prior to each shot – almost on automatic pilot – puts us in the right frame of mind irrespective of the pressure we might be under.

PSYCHOLOGICAL PRINCIPLE
Stick to a standard format. The content is not as important as having something which works for you.

- A pre-shot routine should be repeatable, consistent and incorporated into our action prior to each shot. Even on the driving range. It should become second nature.
- It should seek to generate a level of composure and focus which tunes us in to what we have to do. Notice how professionals each have different pre-shot routines which they follow religiously.
- It should remain of a similar tempo prior to each shot.
- A possible routine might incorporate the following:
  - sit your bag down in the same place
  - assess the shot
  - stand behind the ball
  - visualise the shot you intend
  - check your grip on the club
  - address the ball
  - seat the clubhead behind the ball

– step in with the right foot, then the left
– adjust your stance to feel comfortable
– look at the back of the ball
– look at the target and down to the ball and 'lock in'
– relax the shoulders
– relax your arms with a waggle
– sense or feel the shot
– exhale, which increases relaxation
– use your trigger word to generate the swing

- A pre-shot routine may differ slightly depending on the type of shot, but try to develop a routine which not only generates the right state of mind but can also be repeated effortlessly.

'If you watch someone playing 'in the zone' they are do everything the same – address, tempo, mannerisms. There is a sort of comfort in routine that takes the pressure out of any situation.' Bob Tway

Focus

'It is nothing new or original to say that golf is played one stroke at a time, but it took me many years to realise it.'

Bobby Jones

Key thought

Many events can compete for our attention: we could be worrying about our current score or cursing that last shot; we could be bothered by noisy spectators or moaning about the deteriorating weather. However, the only things that can improve our performance are those which we have control over – such as the present moment.

PSYCHOLOGICAL PRINCIPLE
Focus on your performance and the result will take care of itself

---

- We have control over our swing: focus on that and not the ball. This keeps the mind quiet and free from other distractions.
- Focus on the whole fluid swing, not just the mechanics of the action. Alan Shapiro suggests the swing is too quick a movement for mechanical thoughts to serve any real purpose. He suggests avoiding the tendency to 'join the dots' or attempt to piece together all the miniscule fragments that constitute a complete golf swing.
- However, if you are the kind of golfer who takes comfort from breaking down a process into smaller parts then try using the three static points of the swing as focal points:
    - as you address the ball, think 'fluid'
    - at the top of the backswing, say to yourself 'back'
    - at the end of the swing, say 'stop'

'There was no fussing over the technical details of my swing.'

David Graham after his US Open win in 1981

Keeping in the present

'Golfers are the greatest worriers in the world of sport – due to the time they have on their hands between shots.'

Billy Casper Jnr

Key thought

In perhaps a four hour round of golf the good player might spend only five minutes actually addressing the ball and playing the stroke. There are long periods of inaction with plenty of time to think.

That thinking time can be constructive or destructive.

Destructive thinking occurs when we dwell too much on the past or, indeed, the future. We might over-analyse errors, ponder poor shots, or simply wonder what might have been. Similarly we might – having just completed a good shot – become too self-congratulatory. Thinking too far into the future, imagining the victory ceremony perhaps or the celebratory drink in the bar, can also deflect us from the job in hand.

The sports journalist Simon Barnes noted that 'golf is miserly with its glories, but recklessly generous when it comes to dishing out worry'. We have so much time to think: can we not put that time to more constructive use?

PSYCHOLOGICAL PRINCIPLE
The past doesn't have power over the present unless you surrender that power to it

---

'Walter Hagen once said that every golfer can expect to have four bad shots in a round and, when you do, just put them out of your mind. This is hard to do when you're not even off the first tee when you've had them.'

Jim Murray

Is it possible to have a post-shot strategy to keep our focus and put us in the right frame of mind for the next shot? Here is one possible routine:

1. Remove feelings about the last shot. If you felt it was poor, cough out the feelings of anger, frustration or disappointment. If you felt pleased with the shot, then try to visualise the experience

2. While walking to your ball relax through regular breathing and letting the muscles of your arms, shoulders and chest feel loose.
3. This is not the time to congratulate yourself or lament the errors of the last shot. Put both errors and successes behind you. The next shot is the most important one of all.

'Play the shot at hand. Not the last one or the next one but the one at your feet, in the poison ivy where you put it.'   John Updike.

Switching on and off

'Despite being blessed with the ability to focus intensely on whatever I'm doing through most distractions... I still can't concentrate on nothing but golf shots for the time it takes to play 18 holes.'
                                                                            Jack Nicklaus

Key thought

Most of the time on a golf course is occupied not playing golf strokes. But our focus needs to be at a maximum during the address and the shot itself. We need therefore to be able to switch our concentration on and off as necessary. The most effective focusing strategies are those that minimise the period of optimum concentration, switching totally into focus at the key point.

PSYCHOLOGICAL PRINCIPLE
Concentrate when it counts.

An effective strategy might contain the following:
- When you reach the ball try and step into what Tony Jacklin called a 'cocoon of concentration'; an imaginary bubble through which you can see but distractions cannot impose.
- Review your intentions for the next shot and visualise how you will take it.
- Begin your pre-shot routine.
- Trigger the action you want with a key word or image.
- Watch the shot without judgement and then switch off.
- To switch off, let any feelings over the previous shot quickly dissipate.
- Relax the arms and shoulders.
- Tune into how your body is feeling: we perform best when we feel energised yet physically relaxed.
- Tune into the conditions, the wind, the way the course is playing – but keep your attention off the scorecard.

Jack Nicklaus described moving in and out of focus as like 'moving from peaks of concentration into valleys of relaxation and back again as necessary'.

Focusing on the target

'If you're sure you'll get a bad bounce; if you think you'll land in the water, then you will get a bad bounce and land in the water.'   Gary Player

Key thought

Our focus tends to be drawn to all the potential hazards before us, such as bunkers, the rough, the water or trees. This tends to focus our mind on the hazard even when we try to tell ourselves to ignore it. For example we might instruct ourselves to avoid the tree or keep out of the rough but in doing so we are subtly reminding ourselves of the hazard. We then tend to hit it.

PSYCHOLOGICAL PRINCIPLE
Focus on the target you intend to hit, rather than the hazards you hope to miss.

Don't get bogged down trying to avoid doing something wrong. Work hard at what you have to do right.

- Select the target...
    - driving: a point on the fairway
    - pitching: the green
    - chipping: the flag
    - putting: the hole or, on an undulating green, a point on the camber where the ball is likely to break
- Picture in your mind's eye the shot with the hazard removed.
- Visualise the shot with the ball ending up on the target.

'Golf balls are attracted to water as unerringly as the eye of a middle-aged man to a female bosom.'   Michael Green

Positive thinking

'There isn't a hole out there that can't be birdied if you just think; there isn't one that can't be bogeyed if you stop thinking.'　　　　　　　　　　　　　Bobby Jones

Key thought

If we listen carefully to our inner speech – the instructions and commentary we give ourselves – it can so often be of a negative nature. Thoughts or comments such as 'don't sway'; 'don't move my head'; 'don't hook this one' are negative statements. They draw our focus to the very thing we are trying to avoid. Indeed, our brain seems to ignore the 'don't' instruction and acts on the rest of the statement. So we tend to sway, move our head or hook the next shot.

A positive evaluation improves our chances of more positive thinking – thinking that stresses what it is we are aiming TO DO.

PSYCHOLOGICAL PRINCIPLE
Positive thought generates positive action.

Denis Waitley, in his book *The Psychology of Winning*, suggests ten key aspects of ourselves that can be framed positively. See if you can frame yourself positively in some of the following ways by completing the sentences below. Hold onto the belief as you play the round. Use the successes to validate that aspect of yourself; use the blunders and errors as an opportunity to revisit your belief in readiness for the next shot.

- Awareness: 'I play golf to improve... [eg. my temperament; my approach to problems; my tactical nous]'
- Image: 'As a golfer, I think of myself as... [eg. aggressive; competitive; cultured]'
- Esteem: 'Playing golf makes me feel... [eg. great; alive; relaxed]'
- Control: 'Golf helps me take charge of... [eg. my feelings; my responsibilities]'
- Motivation: 'I am improving as a golfer by... [eg. putting in good practice; studying the game; analysing my round]'
- Expectations: 'On my next round I will... [eg. keep focused; play quality shots; improve on my last round]'
- Direction: 'To improve my golf even further, I aim to... [eg. slow down; stick to my pre-shot routine; get fit]'
- Discipline: 'To ensure I become the best golfer I can, I am going to... [eg. put in good practice time; alter my lifestyle]'
- Dimension: 'Golf is an important part of me because... [eg. I meet colleagues; I keep fit; I feel good]'
- Projection: 'The way I come across to other golfers is... [eg. confident; courteous; good company]'

Healthy thoughts

'Too much is done with too little thought. It must be mind over putter.'

Horton Smith

Key thought

If we act in the way we think, why is it that our mind is so often cluttered with thoughts that help us mess up? Tim Gallwey described our thoughts as 'the enemy within'. On the course we have plenty of time to ponder. Faulty thinking arises from drawing the wrong conclusions from limited evidence; healthy thinking sees an event – good or bad – in perspective.

PSYCHOLOGICAL PRINCIPLE
We are what we think.

Some common errors of thought:
- PUT DOWNS [eg. 'that was a poor shot']. Rather than dwell on the error, analyse the reasons for it happening.
- LIMITING [eg. 'I never do well on this hole; my driving is weak; I'm not sure I've got my grip right']. These construct self-imposed barriers and you end up playing according to those expectations. Work on stretching your expectations: 'This hole gives me chance to improve; to do my best.'
- OVERLOADED – or giving yourself too many instructions. Work on trigger words or key images to generate the actions you want.
- BLACK AND WHITE – or all or nothing thinking. This is where any shot which is less than ideal is perceived as useless. Work on taking a more balanced view: is it true that you always land in the bunker? Look for the exceptions: when was the last time you expected to land in the bunker but didn't? Try humour: is it really the worst shot you've ever played?
- CIRCULAR – the 'what ifs?' [eg. 'What if I drop short of the green? What if I don't make the cut?'] Such thinking is bereft of solutions. Instead, work on your focus. What are you seeking to do next? The next step is under your control, so don't get bogged down in the possible implications of what you might or might not do.

- OVERGENERALISING. This is where you might feel a single error represents the whole picture [eg. 'That one shot ruined my whole round.'] Work on re-framing, so that you might consider the round a success with one small mistake.
- REMEMBER: thinking alone never achieved anything. It needs to be linked with action. Give yourself simple, clear, positive instructions: what are you going to do?

'I'm not saying my golf game went bad, but if I grew tomatoes, they'd come up sliced.'
Lee Trevino

Stay calm

'Bobby Locke did everything quietly and in slow motion.'   Peter Thompson

Key thought

One missed heartbeat or one error – even one thought that it's going too well – and nervousness can creep into our game. Nervousness reveals itself in 3 ways:

1. Somatic – muscular tension; stomach ache; shallow breathing; heart racing; sweating; weakness in the knees; feeling wound-up; 'butterflies' in the stomach.
2. Behavioural – fidgeting; restlessness; rushing shots; increasing pace; disrupted timing.
3. Thoughts – of failure; of making mistakes; 'choking' under pressure; showing yourself up; self-doubt.

Nervousness activates the body. It serves, at a positive level, to prepare the body for confrontation. It is often referred to as 'the fight or flight response'. However, it is also an energy sapper. Inappropriate nervousness is draining. No wonder we can feel exhausted after a tense round.

'Some guys get so nervous the greens don't need fertilizing for a year.'   Dave Hill

---

PSYCHOLOGICAL PRINCIPLE
Calmness counteracts nervousness.

Controlling tension and nerves will conserve energy and help to focus on the task at hand. We should feel a sense of quiet and calm regardless of what goes on around us.

• Before your round take some time to relax. Let all your muscles feel heavy and loose. Let go of any tension. Breathe slowly and regularly, saying 'relax' to yourself each time you breathe out.
• Slow down your pace [we tend to speed up after a bad hole, even sometimes after a good hole]. Develop some slowing down rituals such as practice shots, visualisation, cleaning the ball, taking your clubs out of the bag slowly.
• Move slowly and rhythmically. Tension sets in quicker when we are still. Stretch, walk; shake the hands out before gripping the club.

- Re-frame the feeling. Interpret any signs of nerves as a readiness to compete: the body preparing itself for competition.

'It's a very positive event being nervous. It allows you to do great things.'   Tom Kite

- Relieve tension by tightening the muscles for three seconds and then letting go.
- Positive associations: say 'birdie' to yourself when you breathe out
- Practice relaxing arm, neck and shoulder muscles as you walk between shots. Let the arms feel heavy; let go of the tension in the shoulders.

Relaxed breathing

'Golf is an awkward set of bodily contortions designed to produce a graceful result.'

Tommy Armour

Key thought

When confronted with the unknown, we tend to tighten. Our swing becomes quicker; our rhythm gets disrupted; our breathing becomes rapid and shallow.

Being relaxed tends to counteract such tense, nervous feelings. Being able to relax has many advantages:

It generates a feeling of calmness.

It increases oxygen uptake.

It reduces nervousness.

It enables the muscles to move more quickly, with a greater range of motion.

It slows you down.

It increases a belief in being in control.

It helps focus.

PSYCHOLOGICAL PRINCIPLE
Keep loose and cool, but don't freeze.

Before the shot you can become relaxed by diaphragm breathing [sometimes called centering]. This technique provides a full exchange of all the air in your lungs and allows fresh oxygenated air into the lungs. It further focuses your attention on something you have control over and enables you to achieve a feeling of relaxation. Furthermore, you can achieve all of this without bringing any attention to yourself.

Diaphragm breathing:
1. Stand behind the ball and eye the target.
2. Take a deep, smooth breath in through your nose.
3. Push your stomach out and hold this 'pear shape' for two to three seconds.
4. Let the air out smoothly through the mouth, saying 'relax'.
5. Repeat two or three times.
6. On the final one, relax the main muscle groups [arms and shoulders] by tightening them and then letting go. They should begin to feel weightless.

'When I learned how to breathe, I learned how to win.'　　　　　Tom Watson

It might be useful to have a cue to remind you to take a few diaphragm breaths before each shot. Alan Shapiro suggests that writing a 'B' on your bag can serve as a cue that only you are aware of.

'Under pressure, one of the most important things to do is to breathe.'　　Curtis Strange

Your mind's eye

'I never hit a shot – even in practice – without having a very sharp, focused picture of it in my head.'
Jack Nicklaus

Key thought

Picturing a shot in your mind before playing the stroke can have many beneficial effects. Your memory retains the image and will facilitate the stroke during the moment when it counts. Thus the real shot is a replay of a shot that you have already played in the visual recesses of your mind.

PSYCHOLOGICAL PRINCIPLE
Mental rehearsal encourages automatic pilot.

Visualisation during a round:
- Select the club you want and stand behind the ball.
- Imagine where you want the ball to finish [eg. middle of the fareway; pin high on the green; in the hole].
- Relax with diaphragm breathing. Imagine yourself addressing the ball and, in the correct time frame, play the stroke in your mind's eye concentrating on how it feels. Make it the best stroke possible.
- Visualise the ball's movement towards where you wish it to finish. Picture the flight path, where it lands, how it rolls and where it comes to stop. Make your picture as vivid as possible.
- Effective visualisation is not watching yourself as if in a movie; it is playing the action through in your mind in advance of the act itself.
- Take the shot.
- You can also employ your mind's eye to load your memory bank after a shot you are proud of: visualise what you have just done.

Visualisation at home:
- Practice a shot or iron out an error. Visualise what you would like to see yourself do in order to perform the shot successfully. Practice in your mind's eye until you feel it is mastered.

- Perfect a shot by visualising a top golfer taking the shot. Fade the image of the golfer into yourself so that you are the one who plays the stroke
- Have a dry run. Visualise yourself successfully completing any task you feel less confident about such as teeing off first in front of an audience, confronting a partner who has a tendency to cheat or giving an interview to the press after your championship win.

Test your visualisation skills:

Close your eyes and imagine yourself playing a standard 8 iron pitch to a green where the pin is located on the left edge close to a bunker with the green sloping away. Picture it in as much detail as possible. Then rate your visualisation from 0 [poor] to 10 [excellent] on each of the following qualities:

- Perfection – did the shot land where you wanted?
- Visual – were you aware of the lie? What was the trajectory of the ball? How did it land? Was there backspin? How many bounces did it take?
- Audio – what did the shot sound like: a comforting 'thwock' or a disappointing 'whumph'?
- Kinesthetic – were you aware of the sensation of the club head in your hand and how it registered when you struck the ball?
- Olfactory – were you aware of the smells around you?
- Vividness – was your visualisation in colour?

51

A positive frame of mind

'I'm hitting the driver so good, I gotta dial the operator for long distance after I hit it.'

Lee Trevino

Key thought

Being confident about our ability is central to performing well. Confidence breeds resilience in the face of setbacks. It allows us to shrug off pressure, protects against intimidation and helps to maintain calmness and composure. Doubt is the contrast to feeling confident and we have a tendency, even during a good run of form, to have doubts about it continuing. Keeping doubts at bay and retaining a confidence in our ability is best accomplished, as Tim Gallwey suggested, by 'becoming absorbed in the positives'. A sense of personal mastery can best be gained by considering our golfing accomplishments.

PSYCHOLOGICAL PRINCIPLE
Develop an 'I can do it' attitude: an unwavering belief in your ability to perform.

The Confidence Tower

The Confidence Tower is a means of recording accomplishments. The completed Tower pictured here illustrates the kind of information that might be collected.

It is constructed of six building blocks, each identifying different forms of accomplishment. Building from a solid foundation, complete your own Tower in the following sequence and add to it as you go along:

STRENGTHS   Those aspects of your golfing game that you feel you can accomplish with relative ease. The highly-rated attributes or qualities from your Golfing Profile come under this.

IMPROVEMENTS   Those areas of your game where you feel you have advanced in technique, tactics, attitude, fitness and/or practice.

ACHIEVEMENTS   Those occasions when your personal goal has been reached.

PREVIOUS PERFORMANCE   What are the positive elements of your recent form?

HAVING AN EDGE   What gives you an advantage when you step on to the first tee?

PREPARATION   What has gone well in practice or in the lead up to this round?

52

The Confidence Tower

Having an edge Advantages you have:	Preparation Aspects of preparation which have gone well:
NEVER RUFFLED PUT IN SOME GOOD PRACTICE	QUALITY IRON SHOTS IN PRACTICE CRACKING CARPET PUTTING KNOW THE COURSE
Achievements What I feel proud of:	**Previous performance** Recent success:
REDUCED MY HANDICAP SELECTED FOR THE TEAM NO 3 PUTTS	PRE-SHOT ROUTINE SHOT SELECTION
Strengths My best attributes:	**Improvements** Where I've progressed:
SELF DISCIPLINE SHORT GAME KEEPING RELAXED	BUNKER SHOTS VISUALISATION

- Ensure that your comments are phrased positively and that they refer to characteristics that are under your control.
- Select events that reflect your own strengths and abilities. Avoid making a comparison with other golfers.
- The following quotes undermine confidence as they compare self in a negative manner with someone who has superior ability in a particular area:

'When John Daly hits an iron he takes a cubic yard of Kent as well. His divots go further than my drives.'   David Feherty

- Refer to the Tower before each round, perhaps keeping it in your bag. After each round review what went well and add to your Tower as you recognise further accomplishments.

Play to your strengths

Key thought

Under pressure we have a tendency to revert to type, falling back on skills with which we are familiar. We therefore need to become aware of our strengths; to play to them and use them when we are under pressure. Such perceived strengths become particularly useful when we hit a run of bad form or are having doubts about our ability.

PSYCHOLOGICAL PRINCIPLE
Take ownership of your strengths.

- Identify those qualities on your Golfing Profile where you gave yourself the highest rating. In the example given these were:

  Self-discipline   9
  Iron play   7
  Determination   7

- For each of your strengths you can make them dependable if you:
  1. Identify the times when you show the skill or quality, particularly those times when you have exhibited the skill under pressure. Re-live the highs [eg. the pitch at the flag on the 18th].
  2. Describe in detail how you felt [eg. satisfied; elated].
  3. Describe what it is you did [eg. selected the right club; executed a smooth swing].
  4. Identify what made the difference [eg. my composure].
  5. Re-play the strength through your mind's eye. Visualise yourself exhibiting the quality.
  6. Visualise yourself performing the skill under a pressure situation [eg. in front of a gallery of people].
  7. Describe what it is about you that enabled the shot to be accomplished [eg. 'I showed a professional attitude'].

The lighter side

'The fun you get from golf is in direct ratio to the effort you don't put into it.'　　Bob Allen

Key thought

Is it possible that you're the only one who swings and misses the ball? Or lands in the water hazard? Or hits someone else's ball by mistake? Golf, it would seem, frequently generates feelings of frustration, embarrassment and humiliation. On some days nothing seems to go right. Even during the most difficult times, however, golf also offers us the opportunity to enjoy ourselves. It's a matter of keeping things in perspective.

'My most common mistake at St Andrews is just turning up.'　　　　　Mark James

---

PSYCHOLOGICAL PRINCIPLE
Learning increases as our sense of fun about what is being learnt increases.

Is it possible to construe errors, howlers and setbacks with a glint in the eye?
- Find a metaphor or a vivid way of describing the mistake, such as:

'I was swinging like a toilet door on a prawn trawler.'　　　　　David Feherty

- Make light of it:

'Bob Hope has a beautiful short game. Unfortunately it's off the tee.'

Jimmy Demaret.

- Offer an implausible solution:

'I'd like to see the fairways more narrow. Then everybody would have to play from the rough, not just me.'　　　　　Seve Ballesteros

- Accept your vulnerabiity. During a barren run of form, Guy Hodgson noted that 'the American players have a new name for the 'Great White Shark'; Greg Norman is referred to as 'the Carp.'

- Welcome the variability: it's more interesting than consistency. It offers a chance to understand factors that might influence our play.
- Are there opportunities to re-frame the experience? Landing in the bunker, for example, provides a chance to practice sand shots; a soft putt provides a free practice shot to help on the next hole.
- Are there any positives in being behind, such as being the underdog or lulling your partner into complacency?

'Being seven points behind gives you a definite psychological advantage.'

Alex Murphy

Act as if...

'I like the idea of playing with Nicklaus. Jack plays golf just the way I'd like to.'

Steve Melnyk

Key thought

When we choose to do something in the way someone else does it, we open up the possibility of change and therefore the possibility of improvement. It can be an effective game to play: if we pretend to drive like Tiger Woods we could have a better chance of hitting the ball miles down the fairway.

PSYCHOLOGICAL PRINCIPLE
You may know your limitations but you needn't be limited by them.

Acting is a great learning device. We can sample the experience as if we are someone else. We can adopt the stance of a top golfer and take the shot as if we are that player. To act as if you are a top golfer is a way of developing your potential and breaking the limits you impose on yourself and your performance. It is a form of experimentation.

- When you have a shot to play that generates doubt, think about a golfer who would tend to play it well:
    John Daley driving from the tee
    Phil Mickelson pitching to the green
    Ian Woosnam's swing
    Seve Ballesteros's recovery shots
    Ben Crenshaw's long putting
    Lee Trevino's chip shots
    Bernard Langer's accurate iron shots
    José Maria Olazabel's attacking putting
    Tom Kite's wedge shots
- Get into pretend mode. Play the shot as if you are that golfer. Visualise the player taking the shot and gradually merge yourself into that scene.

59

Personalise your shots

Key thought

Attaching personal meaning, metaphor or images to your shots provides a useful way of focusing. It frees the mind from over-elaborate detail and allows you to make the kind of stroke you want to without technical interference.

- Driving:
  Grip as if you are holding a fledgling bird between your hands.
  Hands in the clouds at the top of the backswing.
  Downswing like a coiled spring.

'You're to turn yourself into material as soft as putty, and then just sort of slop the clubhead through. You hit much further and with less effort.'　　　　　Johnny Miller

- Pitching:
  Pitching the ball as if it is attached to a parachute.

- Chipping:

'When I hit my chip shots right they land, just so, like a butterfly with sore feet.'

Lee Trevino

- Bunker shots:
  Scoop it up like a fried egg from the sand and drop it on the green.
  Imagine the ball is a glass of wine and try landing it on the green without spilling a drop.

- Putting:
  Caress the ball.

'One minute the sword [putter] is making you king, the next it is lacerating you.'

Mac O'Grady

Making the difficult easy

'I shot a wild elephant in Africa thirty yards from me and it didn't hit the ground until it was right at my feet. I wasn't a bit scared – but a four foot putt scares me to death.'

Sam Snead

Key thought

Good scoring is dependent on good putting. They are the shortest shots – and the ones that give most grief. They are also the shots we practise least. Is it possible to make putting easier?

- Imagine the cup as a black hole, creating a vacuum to suck your ball in.
- Imagine rolling the ball into the hole, then let the putter do the same.
- For longer putts, imagine a two-foot circle around the hole and aim for that.
- David Leadbetter suggests practising with a tee for the hole. This not only takes away the pressure of holing it, but when you are out on the course putting for real, the hole appears enormous.

Savour the experience

Key thought

Golf presents many varied and often contradictory experiences. This can be frustrating but equally it might help us to step outside our usual way of thinking and approach the situation differently or more philosophically.

PSYCHOLOGICAL PRINCIPLE

Contradictions present an opportunity to experience the unusual.

Sometimes things don't make sense. The following contradictions are unique to golf. Notice how you experience the situation when you are confronted by it. Is it frustrating or can you take a relaxed view and make it count in your favour?

REMEMBER— THIS IS A CHARACTER BUILDING EXPERIENCE... REALLY... IT IS...

- The two-foot putt counts for as much as the 200-yard drive. Do you treat them with equal seriousness? Would it improve your score to acknowledge them as equally important?
- In a four-hour game you are probably actively hitting the ball for about five minutes. Do you use all the time on the course constructively?
- If you hit with your head down then the ball soars; whereas when you look up the ball is topped.
- The higher the number of the club, the shorter the distance the ball will travel.
- More effort generally means worse results. The harder you try to hit the ball, the less yardage you generally achieve: do you increase your effort or reduce your power when things start to go against you?
- Generally speaking, the slower the start of the swing the further the ball will travel when it is hit. The faster the start of the swing then the less distance the ball will travel.
- Golf is a game where nature [weather, sand, water] is tackled with the most inappropriate set of tools.
- A high level of technical skill is required to hit a stationary ball with no opponent trying to stop you.
- Long stretches of calm are punctuated by short, violent explosions.

Symbolism

Key thought

Golf is rife with symbolism: how it affects you can have a significant impact on your enjoyment of the game. Mulling over the symbolic aspects of the golf game can encourage a playful frame of mind which can in turn help to keep you relaxed during a round.

PSYCHOLOGICAL PRINCIPLE
Symbolism paints an emotional picture of what it represents.

Can you identify the symbolism in your game? More importantly, can you change those that represent negative feelings into positive feelings? Consider the following golfing symbols:

- Your clubs: are they neanderthal, blunt instruments used for battering the ball into small pieces or are they rapier-like weapons that strike the ball cleanly?
- Your bag: is this a symbol of comfort for you? Do its many pockets hold your treasured possessions? Is it an object of attachment?
- Water hazards: do they make you feel like going to the toilet? Do you simply feel that you are in deep water? Or are you struggling to keep your head above water?
- Sand: the bunker could be a symbol of war, something to be fought with. But sand is also a wonderful medium to play in: does it make you as happy as a sand boy?
- The rough: having a rough ride; getting the rough end of the stick. Alternatively, are you able to take the rough with the smooth?
- The green: it can be longed for or loathed. It can make you feel inexperienced (as green as grass) or it can be – with its carefully tended surface – like the Garden of Eden.
- The flag: this might represent submission or surrender. Alternatively it could be a time for celebration (putting the flag out).

Playing with paradox

'The vital thing about a hole is that it should either be more difficult than it looks or look more difficult than it is. It must never be what it looks.' Sir Walter Simpson

Key thought

Doing the unexpected, or contradicting accepted notions, can help focus our awareness on what it is we are doing. We become aware of cues from our body and the information it provides. It can increase our understanding about what underlies the errors in our game.

PSYCHOLOGICAL PRINCIPLE
The paradox is trying out what seems contradictory.
The experiment is noticing the effect.
The lesson is becoming aware of your control over the shot.

- Try strokes with your eyes shut. Set everything up and shut your eyes on the downswing. Notice how it feels. Judge the result of the shot [left/right; short/long] before opening your eyes to notice the effect.
- Try the stroke with 20% less power.
- Try reaching the green with a club two sizes shorter [eg. use a 5 iron when you would expect to reach it with a 3 iron]
- Deliberately make a mistake. Try to hook or slice the ball to a particular point on the fairway in order to get a sense of how it feels.
- Try strokes with your arms/shoulders/fingers tensed.
- Try completing a round ten shots over what you would expect.
- Try playing the back nine first.

Partners

'Give me my golf clubs, fresh air and a beautiful partner and you can keep my golf clubs and the fresh air.'   Jack Benny

Key thought

Few games offer the opportunity for social interaction with your opponent as effectively as golf. This can have both positive and negative repercussions. The key is to be clear about what you would like from your partner; you can then use the situation to your advantage

Before the start of a round decide what you wish to derive from it. Refer to the entry, Game Planning *(pages 20–21)*. You could be playing for fun and relaxation or as part of a business meeting; or you might want to be competitive. Think about letting your partner know this and negotiate a joint agenda.

PSYCHOLOGICAL PRINCIPLE
The chances of being psyched out or psyched up by your partner is greater in golf than in almost any other sport.

Partners can influence our game in many ways. It is important to be aware of such influences and take control. Possible ways we can be 'psyched out' by our partner are:

* By their PRESENCE.

  Most golfers are affected by what other people think of their game. They feel judged. A partner might not have to do anything: their mere presence can instill doubts in our game. It might arise from a sense of inferiority or a wish to avoid humiliation. The only important judge of yourself however, is you. You are the expert on yourself. Focus on the shot at hand, not it's possible outcome or how it might be judged by anybody else.

* By their ADVICE

  If your partner can provide constructive help, use it. If not, then question the wisdom of their advice. Advice is only helpful if you make it so.

'Excuse me madam, would you mind either standing back or closing your mouth. I've lost four balls already.'   Ted Ray

70

- By their NEED

  Does your partner ask you for comments or seek your advice on their game? If you can offer help and it does not distract you from your own game, then this is fine. Golf is a great opportunity for developing genuine feelings of pleasure in what your partner accomplishes.

  However, be very careful of any questions your partner might direct to your own game. Comments like 'your swing is great today'; 'I've never seen you putt so well' – followed usually by 'how is that?' – can be devastating. They direct our focus towards an analysis of our technique. We begin to dissect something that should not be dissected. Our swing is a complete, flowing action and should be free from analysis, particularly if it is working well. As soon as we begin to analyse why something is working, it will deteriorate.

- By their PERFORMANCE.

  Don't worry about how your partner is scoring or performing. This is outside your control. If he hits the wedge brilliantly then be pleased but don't compare your performance with it. Only your game should count to you. In the end you are competing with yourself. You are pitching yourself against the course and the conditions, not against your partner.

- By their BEHAVIOUR

  Your partner's actions are always a source of some distraction. You might be tempted to become caught up in the way they play the game, their attitude to the course or even their dubious scoring. However your partner behaves your shots and strokes are down to you. You will need to focus on your own performance: only that will make a difference to your own game.

- One big advantage of playing with a partner is the opportunity it gives for learning new ideas. We can model aspects of our game on our partner's good points, experimenting with new ways of tackling the many hazards golf throws up. We can learn from their shots: watch their putt, for example, and you can learn how the green is behaving.

A: Why aren't you playing golf with the colonel any more?
B: What! Would you play with a man who swears and curses every shot, who cheats in the bunkers and who enters false scores in his card?
A: Certainly not!
B: Well, neither will the colonel .   Freddie Oliver

Getting to know yourself

'I don't just want to be remembered as a good golfer, I also want people to think of me as a nice guy.'

Fuzzy Zoeller

Key thought

The amount of time spent on the golf course provides ample opportunity for our personality to shine through in ways that it might not in other, shorter sports. It might be regarded as an heaven-sent opportunity to get to know ourselves a little better.

PSYCHOLOGICAL PRINCIPLE
We discover ourselves when things go against us.

Most usually, our behaviour on the golf course reflects how we are in other aspects of life. We take our personality with us. Alan Shapiro suggests golf reveals who we are because we play it in the manner in which we live our lives. According to John Updike, golf offers the opportunity to 'gain insight into the hazardous qualities of our temperament that give us the most difficulty in the course of our daily life.'

Our personality surfaces particularly when we are faced with pressure, and golf can undoubtedly create pressure. How we cope with miss-timed shots, lost balls and missed putts tells us an enormous amount about who we are and how we are likely to react in our everyday life.

'Each player has a golf persona – a predictable character – which the hazards of play subject to unpredictable shifts of fate by turns hilarious, thrilling, heroic and pathetic.'

John Updike

So reflect on how you handle pressure points. What does your reaction tell you about yourself?
- Are you positive, determined, thoughtful, calm?
  These are positive characteristics that you should acknowledge and draw upon whenever you encounter troublesome situations.
- Are you disgruntled, excitable, uninterested, moody?

These are unproductive characteristics in that they will not enhance your ability to overcome pressure. Think what the contrast is to the characteristic in question: eg. active interest rather than uninterested. Try to employ this characteristic the next time you meet a pressure point.

Your golfing self

'Golf is a game in which you are alone with your creator.'   Angus MacVicar

Key thought

We create ourselves. The way we define or picture ourselves can place a limit on our performance. But we can change the vision we have and push back the limits. We can become a better golfer and a better person as part of the same process.

PSYCHOLOGICAL PRINCIPLE
We play according to how we construe ourselves.

From the list of descriptions listed below, select five that best describe how you are on the golf course:

SELF DESCRIPTIONS

perfectionist	competitive	disciplined	patient
optimistic	calm	assertive	sensitive
patient	adventurous	modest	sociable
critical	aggressive	serious	impulsive
unruffled	determined	quiet	cautious
moody	focussed	enthusiastic	ambitious
apprehensive	nervous	over-controlled	lazy

Then select five further words from the same list that best describe how you would like to be [an ideal] on the golf course. On each ideal rate yourself out of ten. Next, consider what you would have to do to be able to rate yourself one point higher on each of the ideal descriptions. How would you have to behave to attain that ideal? Try to be like this on the next round of golf.

Remember that this is your golfing self-image, not necessarily the way you might wish to be in everyday life. You are more than your performance; more than just your handicap. Golf is not what your life is about but rather a game that simulates life.

'I know of no recreation which is a better character builder than golf.'   Tony Jacklin

Your learning style

'One reason golf is such an exasperating game is that a thing learned is so easily forgotten. We find ourselves struggling year after year with faults we had discovered and corrected time and again.'   Bobby Jones

Key thought

We vary in terms of our learning styles. Some benefit from verbal instructions; some prefer to observe; others rely on their sense of what seems correct. Understanding our preferred style and seeking to learn through that channel will increase our chances that a new skill will be 'bedded down' and not forgotten.

PSYCHOLOGICAL PRINCIPLE
If we fail to learn through the way we have been taught, then find new ways to be taught that suit your learning style.

- You are a 'hear and doer' if you can readily translate written words and verbal instructions into action.
  1. You think about what you have learnt from books and from what others have told you.
  2. You keep a diary or notes of your golfing performances.
  3. You make charts to record your performance on each hole.
  4. You use trigger words and positive statements about yourself.

- You are a 'see and doer' if you prefer to observe someone undertaking the skill and can then seek to accurately imitate them in your actions.
  1. You duplicate the actions of others, building on this by watching the professional players on TV and adopting their ways.
  2. You benefit from watching videos and coaches who prefer to show you how to accomplish a particular skill.
  3. You use video to film and review your actions.
  4. You have good visualisation skills.

- You are a 'sense and doer' if you rely on how actions feel and adapt your skill on the basis of this experience.
  1. You attend to certain actions not for the sake of improving them but merely for the sake of experiencing them.
  2. You play by touch.
  3. You benefit from using exercises like 'increasing your awareness'.

Know your feelings

'In golf you've got to keep down your emotions.' Tony Jacklin

Key thought

Golf is a microcosm of life. The whole range of emotions can be experienced on a round of golf. It is important to recognise the cause of those feelings and to acknowledge them, and then to let them go before the next shot. This applies to both positive and negative feelings. If we hold on to them we deplete our energy stores and reduce our overall alertness. We lose our focus and tend to tire towards the end of the round.

PSYCHOLOGICAL PRINCIPLE
Feelings interfere with smooth actions: let them go.

The following are typical feelings on the golf course – sometimes experienced on the same round and occasionally during the same hole. Understand the reasons for the feeling and accept the consequences of a bad shot – but keep your emotions in check. Focus on the next challenge.

1. Excitement. Preparing to elaborate your golfing self: seeing the shot as an opportunity to improve/extend the way you see yourself as a golfer.
2. Exhilaration. Exceeding your golfing self: the shot turned out to be better than you expected.
3. Frustration. Evidence which prevents you improving your golfing self: you keep hooking off the tee, which prevents you considering yourself to have a good drive.
4. Annoyance. Invalidation of your golfing self: you mess up a shot that should have been accomplished.
5. Nervous. The anticipation that you may fail and undermine your golfing self: you might not achieve what you want with a shot, and thus face the possibility of having to revise your view about yourself.
6. Embarrassment. An awareness of acting in ways that may alter how others perceive you.

Disperse the red mist

'I'm getting much better now when I make a mistake. I take a deep breath. I need to do that so I can break the club over my knee.' Bob Hope

Key thought

Golfing skills decompose when we are angry. Making mistakes on the driving range, practice green and on the course is inevitable. Getting mad at ourselves, others or our equipment for doing so is optional. Having a strategy for dissipating our anger before the next shot is crucial. All top golfers leave the error behind. They approach the next shot as if it was the only thing that matters

---

PSYCHOLOGICAL PRINCIPLE
Anger impedes performance. Leave it behind.

Some ideas on overcoming anger before your next shot:
- Thought stopping. This is using a signal such as a verbal command [eg. saying 'stop' forcefully to yourself] or a physical aid [eg. wearing a rubber band around your wrist to snap] to interject and disrupt your angry thoughts.
- Replace angry thoughts with positive ones:
  Picture a calm and relaxing scene, like lying on a tropical beach, and really immerse yourself in that scene. Practice diaphragm breathing. Use positive verbal instructions, such as 'relax'.
- Rate your anger out of ten. The act of doing this depersonalises the anger. It focuses the mind as if the problem were an external one and not a part of you as a person. Try to reduce the rating through relaxing.
- Act as if you are that calm, cool, unruffled professional who glides through errors and readies him or herself for the next shot.
- Perceive the error to be an opportunity to rise to the challenge of combating your anger.
- Perhaps the anger expresses how you really care. Can you take it down a notch or two and see if it energises or motivates you to change what you feel aggrieved about?

'Show me someone who gets angry once in a while and I'll show you a guy with a killer instinct.' Lee Trevino

- Make the error interesting. How could it have been worse? Can you humour your anger? Step outside yourself and see how crazy you look. Tales of failure are far more interesting to talk about in the clubhouse than how well you played. A true cock-up makes for a great story later on.
- Don't bottle up the feeling. Be a sieve, not a jug, when things go wrong. Sift out the essential aspects and let the rest flow away.

'Real golfers, no matter what the provocation, never strike a caddie with the driver. The sand wedge is far more effective.' Huxtable Pippey

Problem? What problem?

'Whenever someone comes to me with a problem, I always ask them what solutions they have thought of.'
                                                                          John Harvey-Jones

Key thought

Sometimes we are the only person to whom we can give advice. After all, how often do we accept the advice of others? Sometimes we seek advice merely to confirm what we want to do anyway: this is not taking advice it is giving ourselves the licence to behave as we want to behave.

We are also inclined to look for magic answers whereas in reality they very rarely exist. We are usually better off not looking for answers but looking for ideas to try out. In this way we can experiment with new ventures and assess their impact and result. Was it a poor idea – in which case we can bin the idea – or was it a cracking idea which puts you on track for solving the problem?

PSYCHOLOGICAL PRINCIPLE
You know what the problem is and you have the resources to solve it.

Solutions come from asking questions of ourselves: we are looking for good questions, not good answers. Apply the following questions to the problem:

- Understand it. When does it happen? What is it you do?
- Name it. Can you give it a name, such as 'inconsistency'; 'stiffness'; 'guilt'? Once named, a problem becomes more manageable. You can perhaps kick it around a little or knock it out of shape. With non-golfing problems you might bin it or bag it – leaving it in the boot of your car – and return to it once you have finished the round.
- Interrogate it. Ask the problem some stiff questions: what is its impact on you? What would you be like without it? What lurks behind the problem [embarrassment; inferiority; anger; being technically inept]?
- Rate it. Put it on a scale of zero to ten, where zero is no problem and ten is absolutely massive. The first number that comes into your head is usually the most accurate.

- Undermine it. Try to figure out when the problem has a lower rating than that which you just gave it. At such times you are asserting yourself over the problem. What is it that you are doing differently at these times?
- Take control of it. What would move the problem one point lower down the scale? What would you do to ensure this happens?
- Enlist support. When you get stuck for ideas in tackling the problem, work out how somebody else [a friend; partner; admired golfer; film star; cartoon figure] might tackle the issue.
- Solve it. What is the smallest sign of the problem improving? Imagine yourself without the problem: what is it you are doing and how come you can be like this?

'Tee the ball high. Years of experience have shown me that air offers less resistance to dirt.'

Jack Nicklaus

A philosopher on the course

'The mind is something to think with, not for worrying.'   Anonymous

Key thought

By its very nature, golf is impossible to master. Recognise this, but don't become immersed in what might have been. Sometimes we lose ourselves in the past, dwelling on the 'if only...' ('if only I didn't take 7 on the 9th I'd have beaten my best score'). It is of course possible to revisit the past, but during the game it should only warrant the briefest of thoughts – of acceptance – before you regain your focus on the next shot. What's done is done. It's important to remain philosophical.

PSYCHOLOGICAL PRINCIPLE
Accept what's gone; focus on the present.

A few useful approaches to philosophical golf:
- Shrug off the bad shot. It is the next one that is the most important. All golfers make bad shots; the best golfers re-focus and keep the bad shots to a minimum. Note how often the top golfers make a birdie on the hole following one on which they drop a shot.

'The only thing you can control is your attitude towards the next shot.'
Mark McCumber

- Don't seek to play perfect golf. If you're looking for perfect golf you are looking on the wrong planet. Maybe sometimes we have to play ugly golf. Indeed, most golf shots are miss-hits of a kind; they are rarely perfect even at a professional level. It is the quality of the miss-hit that separates good scoring from bad.
- Try not to judge the error. It happened; it might happen again sometime. Those who don't make errors live in a state of fear. Take credit for screwing up and yet having the capacity to battle on.

- Play without knowledge of the score. It is the performance which counts, not the outcome.
- Try to accept adversity with dignity and an ironic half-smile playing across your lips.

Take response-ability

'I would like to speak to whoever is in control of my life, and suggest some improvements.'
Ashley Brilliant

Key thought

There is a tendency within some of us to take credit for the successes and ignore the failures. Thus we credit ourselves when a shot reaches an intended target [eg. 'my swing is smooth; I'm on song today']. But we blame the circumstances when we put the ball out of bounds or in the water [eg. 'the wind caught the ball; who put that bunker there?').

Golf is a game we play against ourselves. There is no one to blame for our errors except ourselves. If we credit ourselves with success; we similarly have to take responsibility for our mistakes.

'Man blames fate for other accidents but feels personally responsible for a hole in one.'
Martha Beckman

Respsonse-ability is having the ability to choose our response. It is not about blaming others, or circumstances, for our behaviour.

PSYCHOLOGICAL PRINCIPLE
Take charge of events; don't let them take charge of you.

- Blaming things we have no control over prevents us from doing anything about it. It may feel better to blame the bad lie but it will not help us in developing a better response to bad lies in the future.
- Make an honest assessment of what part you played in the error and take control over it.
- There is much that we do not have control over, such as the weather, the speed of the green, our partner's behaviour. It may be possible to assert some control over such uncertainties by asking: 'what's the best way I have of coping with this?' Practice visualising yourself successfully handling such a situation.
- If something really is outside your control, then don't be distracted or worried by it. Let it take care of itself.
- After an error, take control. Don't blame the circumstances. What can you learn from the mistake? Phrase your analysis in terms that enable you to learn from it. Eg. 'I should have ...'.
- Make any shots, good or bad, work for you in some way. A good shot might confirm your strength in that area and build your confidence. A poor shot can inspire you to perform better.

Dealing with pressure

'Pressure is when you're playing for $10 and you don't have a dime in your pocket.'

Lee Trevino

Key Thought

All events are open to interpretation. We make sense of them by what we read into them. What is the difference between a six-foot practice putt on the back lawn and a six-foot putt on the 18th to birdie the hole and win the club tournament? The difference is related to how much baggage we anticipate coming with the outcome.

'If this were any other tournament than the Masters I'd have shot a 66. But I was choking out there. The Green Jacket plays castanets with your knees.'

Chi Chi Rodriguez

The environment can create the context, but not the pressure. The experience of pressure comes from the perception of the event and its repercussions – not the event itself. It's still only a six-foot putt.

PSYCHOLOGICAL PRINCIPLE
It's only pressure if you think of it that way.

Addressing pressure:
- Be prepared. Stick to your game plan; keep to your pre-shot routine; run through the way you plan to play each hole; visualise the shots and your swing; visualise the way you want to play and imagine the most 'pressurised' atmosphere you can – with a large crowd watching, for example.
- Relax, stay calm; maintain your composure.
- Stay positive. Refer to your confidence tower.
- Stay focused on what you intend to do.
- Slow down.
- Practice under pressure to see how it feels. Play the hardest tournaments you can; increase the size of the winnings when playing a partner; play two shots lower than your handicap.

'Putting is clutch city. Usually my putting touch deserts me under pressure. From five feet in to the hole you are in the throw-up zone.' Dave Hill

Dealing with defeat

'Failure is what makes succeeding so sweet. In golf failure is a great thing: an absolutely necessary thing.'

Greg Norman

Key thought

Focusing on defeat traps you in the outcome and places you in the role of loser. Improvement comes from focusing not on the outcome but on what you can control and change.

PSYCHOLOGICAL PRINCIPLE
Winners are those who do their best.

• Put the result in context:

        Does it put your self-worth on the line?

        Where does it sit with your overall targets?

        Is it the worst thing that ever happened?

To fail means you messed up this time. It does not imply that you are a failure. S.I. Hayakawa suggest we notice the difference between what happens when a man says to himself 'I have failed three times' and what happens when he says 'I am a failure.'

'I didn't lose a war. Nobody died. I lost a game of tennis that's all.'

Boris Becker

• What can be learnt:

        Analyse your scorecard; consider each shot you made.

        What would you do differently?

        What would you ensure happens next time?

        Errors are valuable if we build from them.

• Did you do yourself justice?

        What targets were reached?

        What successes were accomplished?

Pursuing your limits

'The only limitations are mental; you can do anything you want.'

Daley Thompson

Key thought

We often play within a 'comfort zone' where we match our expectations and are driven by a desire not to fail. This can lead to an avoidance of risks and the pursuit of mediocrity rather than excellence.

PSYCHOLOGICAL PRINCIPLE
To risk success might mean having to re-evaluate the way you see yourself.

GO FOR IT:

G Give yourself permission to succeed. Enjoy yourself. Be as good as possible. Go beyond what you have done before.

O This is an Opportunity to project yourself: present yourself in a way that you would like.

F Focus on performance, not the outcome. Get the performance right and the outcome will take care of itself.

O Options present choices. Use whatever opportunity presents itself to your advantage.

R Re-frame limitations as frontiers. Limitations are self-imposed; frontiers are there to be pushed back.

I Be an inspiration to yourself.

T Take the risk of winning: that's your choice

'Muirfield without a wind is like a lady undressed: no challenge.'   Tom Watson

The perfect golfer?

Why don't I improve?

Key thought

Improvement and progress can be slow, not because we find learning new things difficult but because change itself is difficult. Change may feel unnatural and we therefore stick or revert to what we know. We end up repeating what we have always done simply because it feels comfortable, even though it might not be good for us.

We might choose to feel happy with how we are: 'I always hook'; 'I'm a terrible putter' because that is how we see ourselves. Better to do this than risk improvement because then we will have to re-evaluate the way we see ourselves. Could you see yourself as someone who has a lethal putt?

PSYCHOLOGICAL PRINCIPLE
Change is inevitable; growth is optional.

Whenever you are struggling to improve, ask yourself the following:

1. What is it (the ideal) I am trying to do?
2. What are the benefits of the ideal? This provides the reasons for wanting to improve: the motivation.
3. What are the disadvantages of being like the ideal? This provides the reasons for not changing: the resistance

You might then complete the grid on the opposite page to improve your understanding as to why improvement is difficult.

	Benefits	Disadvantages
as I am now [eg. erratic swing]	R retreat to the familiar in the comfort zone [eg. it works about 6 out of 10 times]	M wish for change [eg. I know it looks ugly]
as I hope to be [ideal] [eg. smooth swing]	M as I hope to be [eg. less tense across the chest]	R sense of loss [eg. I might get some initial success then revert to old habits]

M squares indicate reasons for wanting to change (motivation).
R squares indicate why you might resist change (resistance).

Index

Act as if 58,60

Awareness of actions 26, 51, 68, 77

Awareness of performance 27

Body awareness 25

Calmness 10, 32, 46, 48, 52, 89

Concentration 10, 38

Confidence 10, 11, 13, 15, 52, 87, 89

Control 10, 13, 16, 17, 20, 34, 43, 45, 48, 49, 53, 68, 70, 83, 87

Creativity 9, 11

Decision making 11, 22

Determination 15

Diaphragm breathing 49, 50, 80

Discipline 15, 43

Exceptions 44

Expectations 43, 44

Externalising 12

Feedback 24

Focus 15, 28, 32, 34, 36, 38, 40, 45, 46, 48-50, 60, 68, 70, 71, 84, 89, 90, 92

Key images 30, 31, 38, 44

Overcoming pressure 32, 33, 49, 52, 54, 55, 63, 73, 88, 89

Performance Profile 14, 15, 17, 52, 55

Planning 15, 20, 21, 70, 89

Positive thinking 13, 17, 42, 43, 57, 77, 80

Post-shot strategy 36

Pre-shot routine 18, 19, 32, 33, 38, 89

Re-frame 45, 47, 57, 92

Relaxation 11, 13, 33, 37, 38, 46-50, 64, 66, 80, 89

Self-awareness 11, 13, 43

Self-dimension 43

Self-direction 43

Self-esteem 43

Self-image 43, 74, 75, 78

Self-projection 43, 92

Setting goals 16, 52

Thought stopping 80

Trigger words 28, 29, 33, 38, 44, 77

Visualisation 11, 19, 32, 36, 38, 40, 46, 50, 51, 55, 58, 61, 77, 87, 89

Also by Richard Butler

Sports Psychology in Action (1996) ISBN 0 7506 2436 1

Performance Profiling (1996) ISBN 0 947850 36 8

Sports Psychology in Performance (1997) ISBN 0 7506 2437 X